Silly Science Tricks

(With Professor Solomon Snickerdoodle)

Designed by Bill Foster of Albarella & Associates, Inc.
and Peter Hautman
Edited by Kristin Ellerbusch

Distributed to schools and libraries
in the United States by
ENCYCLOPAEDIA BRITANNICA EDUCATIONAL CORP.
310 South Michigan Ave.
Chicago, Illinois 60604

Library of Congress Cataloging-in-Publication Data

Murray, Peter, 1952 Sept. 29-
Silly Science Tricks / written by Peter Murray.
p. cm.
Summary: Presents scientific tricks and
experiments such as blue celery,
weird water, and rubber bones.
ISBN 0-89565-976-X
1. Science — Experiments — Juvenile literature.
2. Scientific recreations — Juvenile literature.
(1. Science — Experiments.   2. Experiments.
3. Scientific recreations.)   I. Title.
Q164.M87   1992
507'.8 — dc20   92-18903
                                              CIP
                                               AC

Silly Science Tricks

(With Professor Solomon Snickerdoodle)

Written by Peter Murray

Illustrated by Anastasia Mitchell

another Umbrella book

THE CHILD'S WORLD

The Upside-down Professor

The other day I found Professor Solomon Snickerdoodle behind his laboratory hanging upside down from an apple tree. He was wearing a helmet made of tinfoil.

"Good morning, my young friend," he said. "You are just in time to observe my latest experiment. And with that he let go and fell on his head.

"Ouch!" said the professor. He sat up, rubbing his head. The helmet, which now looked very much like a ball of crumpled-up tinfoil, lay on the grass beside him. "It seems my helmet has failed me."

"The experiment has failed?" I asked.

"Wrong! The experiment is a success! I have proven that tinfoil is not strong enough to make a good helmet!"

The professor always looks on the bright side. I asked him what were his all-time-best experiments.

"The best idea I ever had was the *Turn Broccoli into Cookies* experiment," he said. "Too bad it didn't work."

"I only want to know about experiments that work," I said.

"Hmmm," said the professor, thinking hard. "I tell you what. Come back tomorrow and I'll show you a few experiments that *always* work!"

Blue Celery and Two-tone Flowers

The next day I was back at Professor Snickerdoodle's laboratory. The professor was wearing a strange-looking flower in the lapel of his lab coat. It looked like a carnation, but it was green on one side and red on the other.

"What a weird-looking flower!" I said.

The professor smiled, then took a piece of celery out of his pocket and took a bite out of it. The celery was blue!

"Are you sure you should eat that?" I asked.

"Of course," said the professor. "Would you like to know the secret of turning celery blue?"

How to make a stalk of celery turn blue:

1. Put ten drops of blue food coloring in a glass containing one inch of water.

2. Cut the bottom off a stalk of celery and put it in the glass. Leave it overnight.

3. The next day, you will have blue celery!

"But what about the red and green flower in your lapel?" I asked.

"Same principle," the professor said. "But to make the flower two different colors, you have to do one more thing."

How to make a two-tone carnation:

1. Put two small glasses next to each other. Pour one inch of water into each glass.

2. Add ten drops of red food coloring to one glass, and ten drops of green food coloring to the other glass.

3. Using a very sharp knife (ask an adult for help with this), slit the stem of the carnation.

4. Put half of the stem in the red water and half in the green water.

Tomorrow you will have a two-tone carnation!

How it works:

Plants have tubes called "xylem" that pull water up the stem to the leaves and flowers. All plants, from the tallest trees to the smallest blades of grass, use xylem tubes to move water.

When you put celery in colored water, the food coloring is drawn up the stalk with the water. If you cut the stalk in half, you can see the xylem tubes as blue dots.

The carnation stem contains xylem tubes, just like the celery stalk. When you slit the stem lengthwise, you separate the tubes into two groups. Each side of the stem carries water to a different side of the flower.

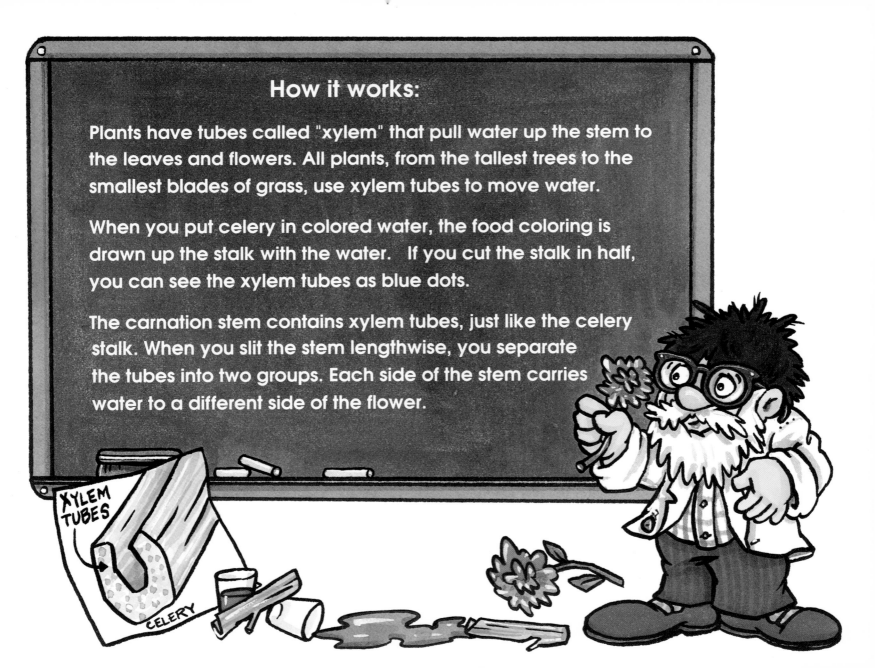

XYLEM TUBES

CELERY

Weird Water

Next, the professor showed me three large bowls full of water on his kitchen table. "This experiment teaches you the difference between hot and cold," he explained.

"But everybody knows the difference between hot and cold!" I said.

"Wrong again!" declared Professor Solomon Snickerdoodle. And with that, he told me to put my left hand in the red bowl and my right hand in the blue bowl.

"Keep your hands in the water," he said. "Now, do you know which bowl is full of hot water and which is full of cold water?"

That was easy! The red bowl was full of hot water. The water in the blue bowl was ice cold.

"Very good," said the professor. "Now put *both* hands in the yellow bowl."

When I put both hands in the yellow bowl, I let out a shout! My left hand told me that the water was cold, and my right hand told me that it was hot—*but they were both in the same bowl!*

"That, my young friend, is what I call *Weird Water!*"

How to make Weird Water:

1. Fill one bowl with hot tap water. It should be hot, but not so hot that you can't hold your hand in it.

2. Fill a second bowl with ice water. Put a bunch of ice cubes in it to make it really cold.

3. Fill a third bowl with water at room temperature. Set it between the other two bowls and say, "You're weird, water!" (If you feel silly talking to a bowl of water, you can skip this part.)

4. That's all there is to it!

LOOKS PRETTY EASY!

HOT WATER

Cold WATER

ROOM TEMP. WATER

How it works:

"Weird Water" is, of course, just plain water. The experiment only works when you have first made one hand very warm, and the other hand very cold. "Weird Water" feels hot to one hand and cold to the other because each hand compares the temperature to what it felt a moment ago.

If you held your hands in the hot and cold water bowls, then put your hands on your face instead of into the water, you would get the same strange feeling in your hands—your face would feel hot to one hand and cold to the other. Does that mean you have a weird face?

You can't always trust what your sense of touch tells you!

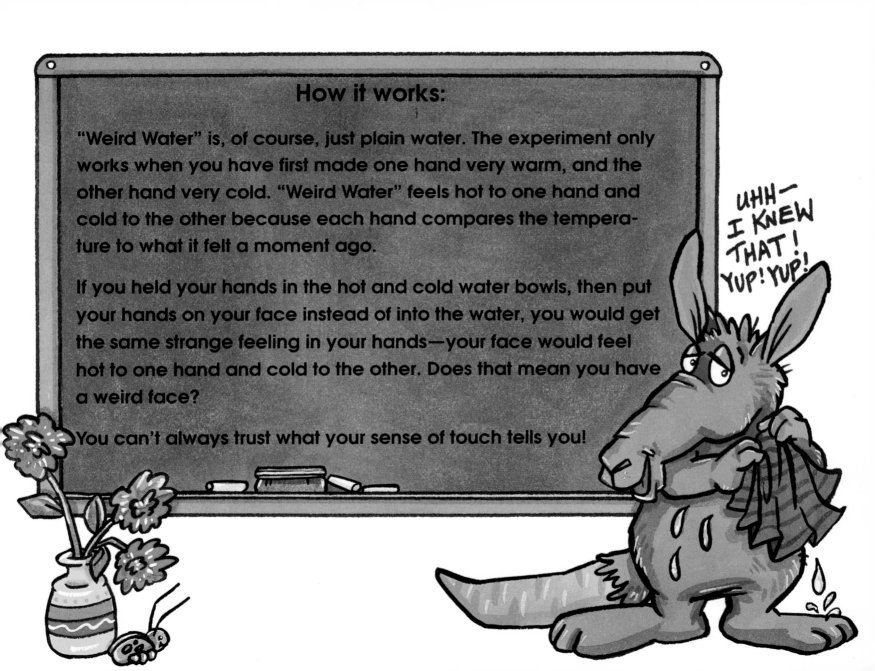

Quicksand

"Are you now convinced that I am a great scientist?" asked the professor.

"Not quite," I said.

"That is only because I have not yet shown you how to make your own quicksand!"

The professor got a box from his pantry and shook a few handfuls of white powder into a big bowl, then added some water. After stirring it a few times, he set it on the floor.

"It looks like a bowl full of milk," I said.

"Observe," said the professor. He produced a rubber ball and dropped it on the "quicksand." I jumped back, thinking I was going to get splashed, but the ball bounced off the white surface as if it were rock hard.

"That looks more like cement than quicksand," I said.

"Wrong again!" said the professor. He set the rubber ball on the surface of the "quicksand" and we watched it sink quickly from sight!

How to make quicksand:

1. Mix one cup of cornstarch with 3/4 cup water.

2. The mixture should be very thick. If it seems too soupy, add more cornstarch.

3. Cornstarch quicksand is very strange feeling stuff. You can pick up chunks of it, but as soon as you get a handful, it seems to melt in your hands!

I cup+ CORNSTARCH
3/4 cup WATER

ANY ANTS IN THERE?

The Magic Balloon

"Now I'm going to show you my magic balloon experiment," said Professor Snickerdoodle.

He went into the next room and closed the door. A few minutes later he came out holding a limp balloon. He tied off the end of the balloon.

"Professor," I said, "You are supposed to blow the balloon up *before* you tie it off!"

NOW WHAT??!

"Wrong again, my young friend!" Holding the balloon in one hand, the professor started to blow on the thumb of his opposite hand.

To my amazement, the balloon began to grow!

AARDVARKS JUST LOVE ANTS!!!

I AM NOT AN ANT!

How to inflate a balloon by blowing on your thumb:

1. Take one teaspoon of baking soda and roll it tightly into a tinfoil tube. Twist the ends closed.

2. Insert the tube into a large balloon.

3. Fill the balloon with vinegar and tie it off.

4. When you are ready to make the balloon inflate, break the tinfoil tube inside the balloon and start blowing on your thumb. The balloon will slowly inflate!

1 TIN FOIL
BAKING SODA
ROLL

2 TUBE
BALLOON

3 VINEGAR
THE TUBE INSIDE BALLOON

4 VINEGAR
BREAK TUBE

Rubber Bones

"And now, my famous rubber-chicken experiment," said the professor, taking a glass filled with clear liquid down from a shelf. Something was floating in the liquid. The professor took it out with his fingers, shook it off, and held it out.

It was the wishbone of a chicken.

"Make your wish," said the professor.

EXCUSE ME — BUT WHERE DID YOU GET THAT BEAUTIFUL WISHBONE?

"I wish for a plate of cookies," I said as I grabbed the other end of the wishbone and pulled. But the bone wouldn't break—*it stretched!*

The professor laughed, then tied the wishbone in a knot and gave it to me.

"When it dries, it will get hard again and no one will be able to figure out how you tied it in a knot!"

How to turn a chicken bone into rubber:

1. Put a chicken bone in a glass full of vinegar. Wishbones work best, but any small bone will do.

2. Let it soak for two days, then pour off the vinegar.

3. Add some fresh vinegar and let it soak for two more days.

4. The chicken bone will become as soft and flexible as rubber!

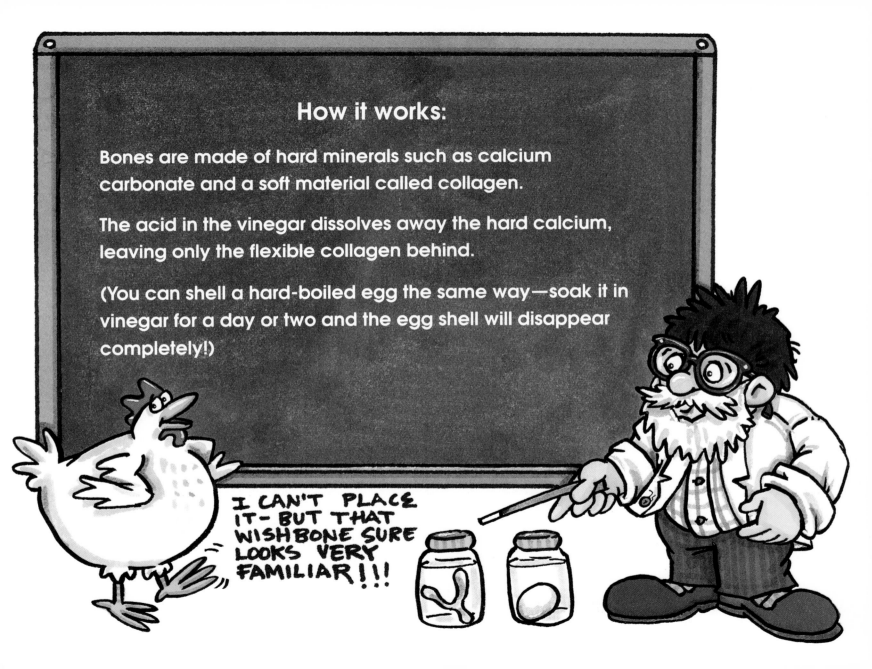

Invisible Ink

"That rubber wishbone trick was pretty impressive, Professor," I said. "But I still wish I had some cookies."

"I have no cookies," he said, handing me a sheet of paper. "Here is a secret message for you."

I looked at the paper. It was blank!

"It doesn't say anything," I said.

"Wrong again!" exclaimed the professor. "Take it home and iron it."

"You mean like you would iron a shirt?"

"Precisely!"

When I got home I had my mom help me iron the blank sheet of paper. A message began to appear in brown letters:

WOULD THAT HAPPEN TO BE CHOCOLATE·COVERED ANT COOKIES?!! YUM!!

PROFESSOR SOLOMON SNICKERDOODLE INVITES YOU FOR COOKIES AND MILK TOMORROW AT THREE O'CLOCK SHARP!

I went back to the professor's laboratory the next day at three o'clock and asked him how he had made the invisible ink.

How to make invisible ink:

1. Squeeze the juice out of half a lemon.

2. Dip a small brush or toothpick into the lemon juice and write your message on a piece of white paper.

3. When the lemon juice dries, the message will be invisible.

4. To read the message, heat the paper using an iron or by holding it close to a hot light bulb.

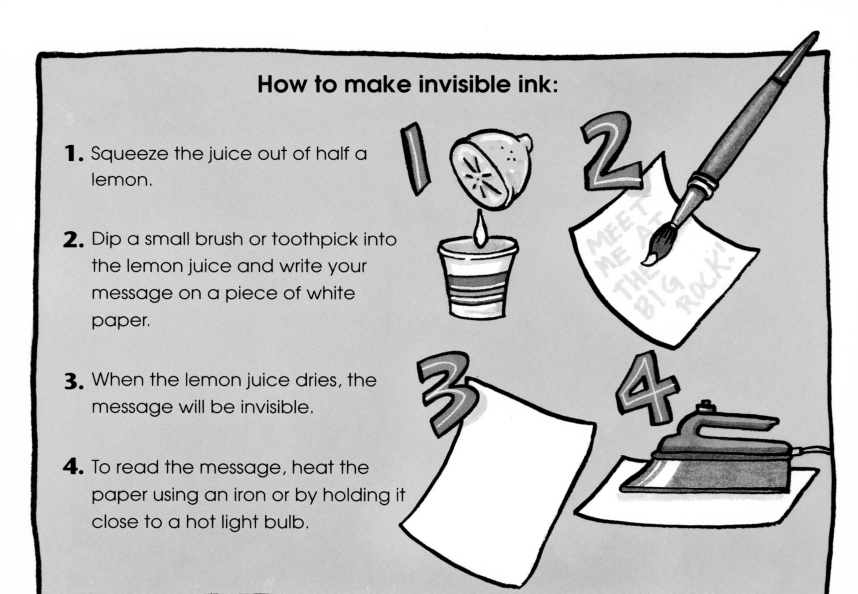

The Disappearing Cookie

After telling me how to make invisible ink, the professor put out a plate of cookies and two glasses of milk.

"*Now* who is the world's greatest scientist?" he asked.

"Professor Solomon Snickerdoodle, you are the greatest!" I said, munching on a cookie. "And your cookies are not bad, either!

"Thank you, my young friend!"

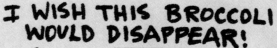

I WISH THIS BROCCOLI WOULD DISAPPEAR!

We ate cookies until only one remained. Of course, we were both too polite to take the last one.

I said, "And now, professor, I would like to show you one of *my* experiments! How to turn one cookie into two cookies!"

"That sounds like a wonderful experiment," said the professor.

"Close your eyes for a moment."

The professor closed his eyes.

A moment later, when he opened them, the last cookie was gone!

"Your experiment has failed!" exclaimed the professor.

"Wrong!" I said, my mouth full of cookie. "The experiment was a success! We now know it is impossible to turn one cookie into two!"

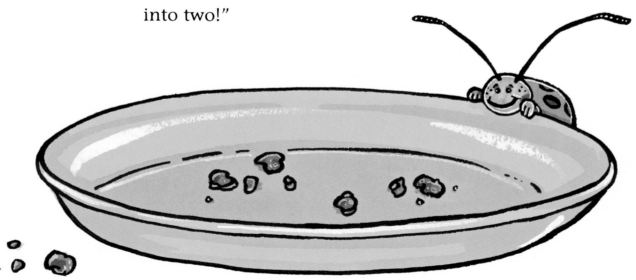